MAKE YOUR OWN

PAPER ROLL PEACOCK

BY MARI BOLTE

PEBBLE

a capstone imprint

Published by Pebble, an imprint of Capstone
1710 Roe Crest Drive, North Mankato, Minnesota 56003
capstonepub.com

Library of Congress Cataloging-in-Publication Data is available on the Library of Congress website.
ISBN: 9780756580742 (hardcover)
ISBN: 9780756580698 (paperback)
ISBN: 9780756580704 (ebook PDF)

Summary: Make a colorful feathered friend! Grab a few simple art supplies and follow the easy steps and clear pictures to create your very own paper roll peacock.

Editorial Credits
Editor: Erika L. Shores; Designer: Heidi Thompson; Media Researcher: Jo Miller;
Production Specialist: Tori Abraham

Image Credits
Capstone: Karon Dubke: all project photos, supplies; Shutterstock: Jenny Schuck, 22, rickyd, 5, Rusalka379, 23

Printed and bound in China. 5834

TABLE OF CONTENTS

Fancy Feathers 4

What You Need 6

What You Do 8

Take It Further 20

Glossary 24

About the Author 24

Words in **BOLD** are in the glossary.

FANCY FEATHERS

Peacocks are nature's show-offs. Their feathers can be 6 feet (1.8 meters) long. You probably don't have space for a life-size peacock. But you can craft a whole **flock** with a few supplies. Follow the steps in this book to make a fancy friend dreamed up by you.

WHAT YOU NEED

- blue paint

- paintbrush

- empty toilet paper roll

- glue

- googly eyes

- scissors

- orange, light green, green, and purple paper

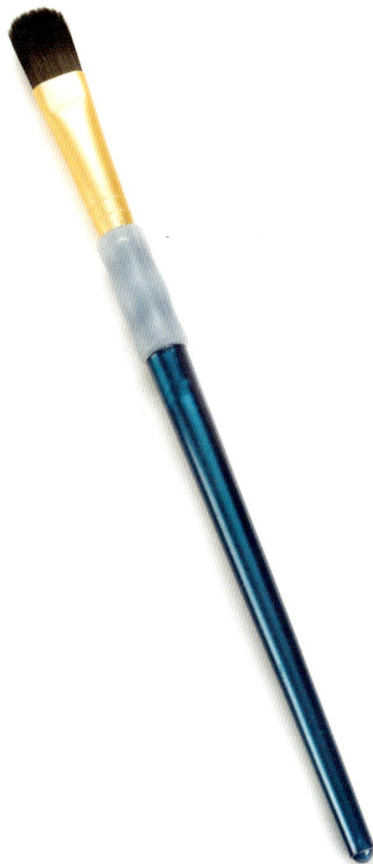

WHAT YOU DO

STEP 1

Paint the paper roll. Let the paint dry.

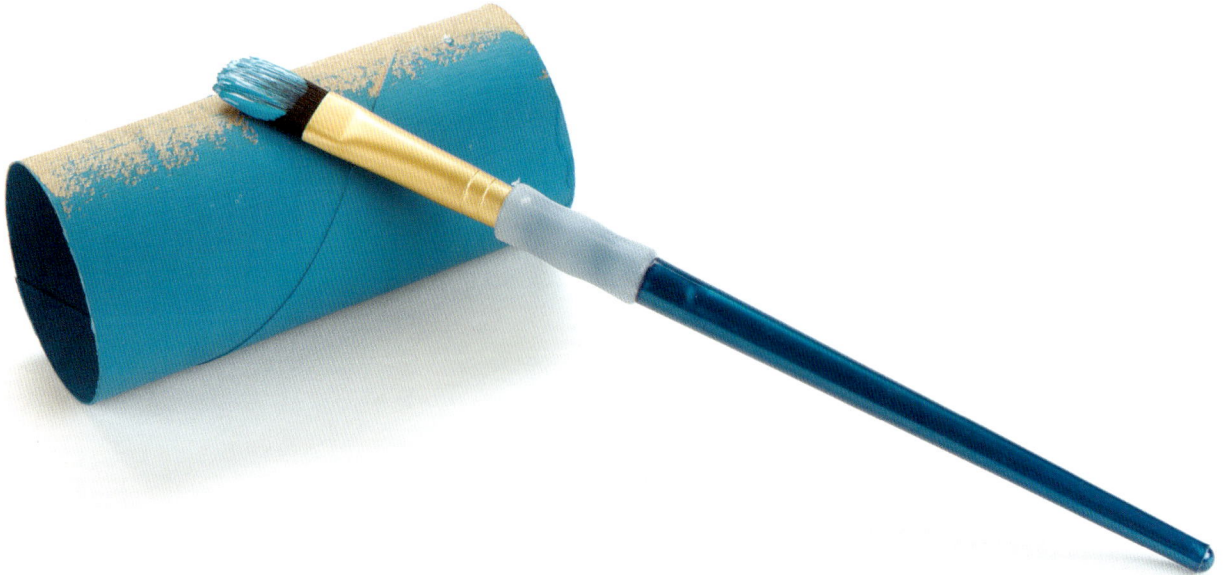

Glue on googly eyes.

STEP 2

Cut out a small triangle from the orange paper. This is your peacock's **beak**.

Glue it onto the paper roll. It should be just below where you added the eyes.

STEP 3

Cut thin strips from the long side of the green, light green, and purple paper. The strips should be about two fingers wide.

Cut four strips from the green and light green paper. Cut out three purple strips.

STEP 4

Glue one end of a green paper strip to the back of the peacock. Glue it near the bottom of the paper roll.

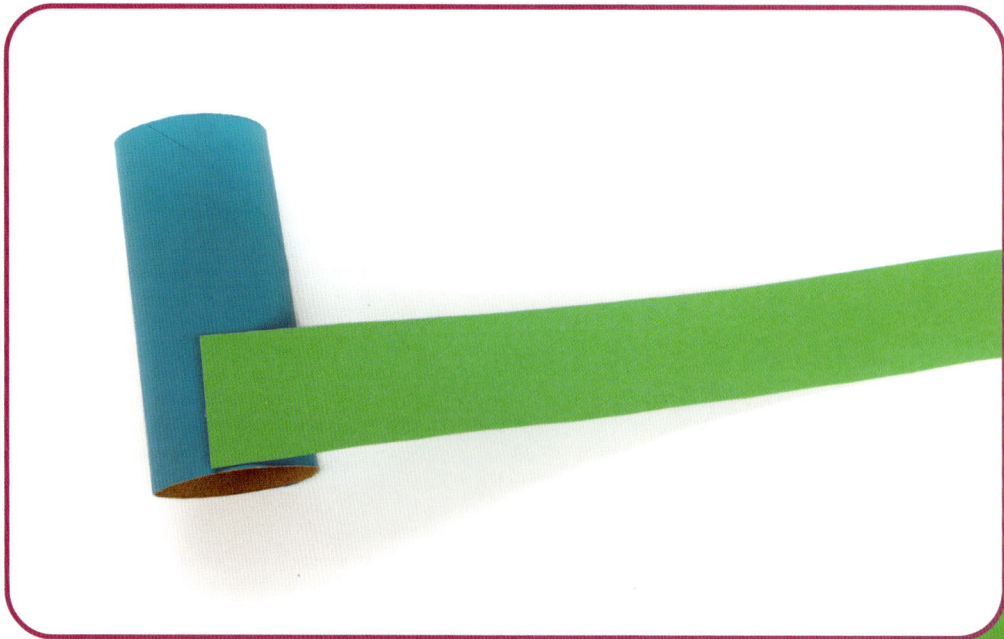

Glue another green strip to overlap the first one. Then add two light green strips in a slight V shape.

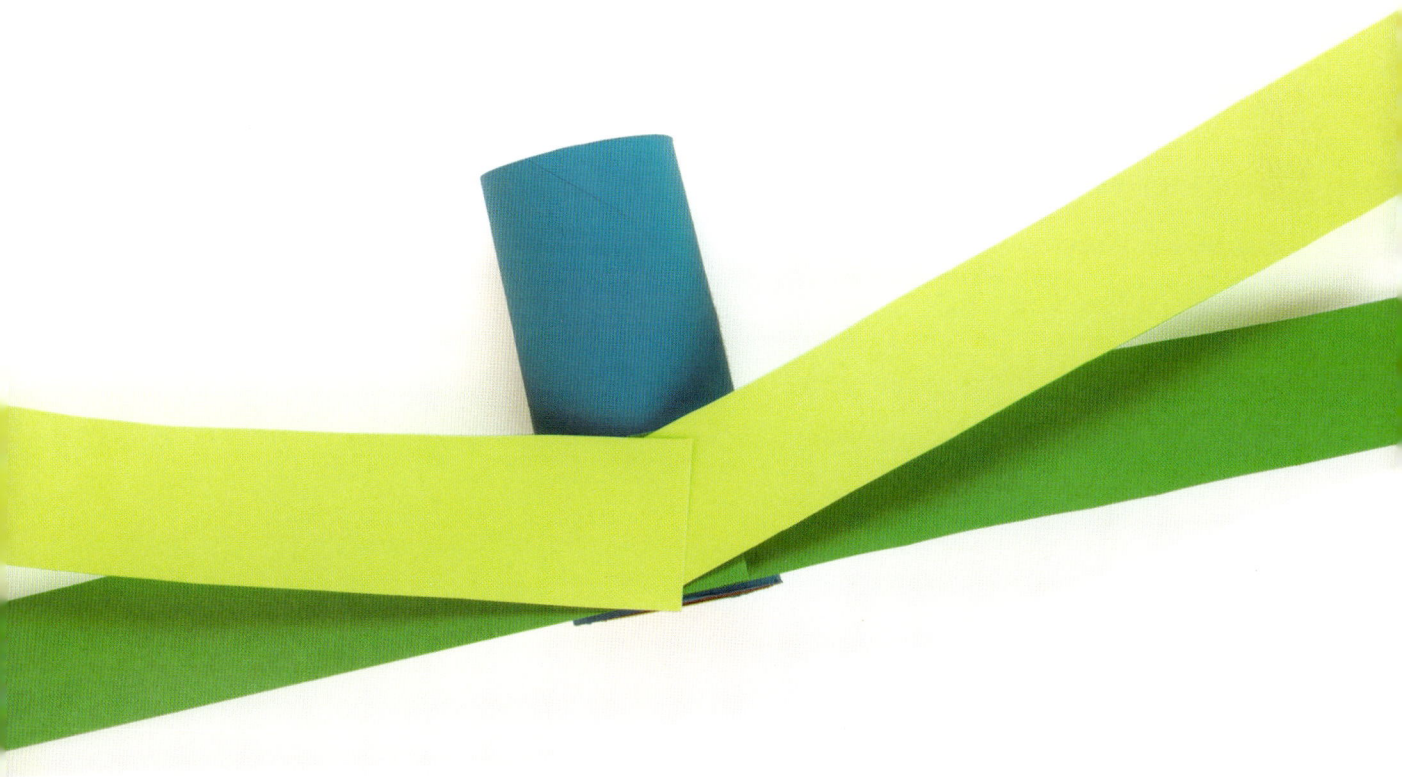

STEP 5

Keep adding paper strips. Add purple next, then green, and then light green. The strips should fan out, like the sun's rays. End with purple.

STEP 6

Loop the paper strips so the short ends touch.

Glue the ends together.

TAKE IT FURTHER

Peacock feathers have dots on them. They are called **eyespots**. Draw black circles on the loops of paper.

Get silly! Add googly eyes to the circles.

Peacocks can be many colors. Use **shades** of pink or purple instead of blue. You could even make a peacock that is all white.

For a rainbow look, use paint chip cards. Find them at stores that sell paint. Cut the cards into strips. You won't need to loop them.

GLOSSARY

beak (BEEK)—the hard front part of the mouth of birds

eyespot (EYE-spot)—a dark spot on a peacock's feather that looks like the eye of a larger animal

flock (FLAHK)—a group of the same kind of animal

shade (SHAYD)—the lightness or darkness of a color

ABOUT THE AUTHOR

Mari Bolte lives in the woods surrounded by books, animals, and crafting supplies. When she's not writing or editing books for kids, she's tromping through the woods looking for what's waiting to be discovered.